Hinduism Made Easy

Hindu Religion, Philosophy and Concepts

KU-208-637

Shalu Sharma

Other books by Shalu Sharma

Hinduism For Kids: Beliefs And Practices
Buddhism Made Easy: Buddhism for Beginners and Busy People
Religions of the World for Kids
Mother Teresa of Calcutta: Finding God Helping Others: Life of Mother Teresa

Hare Krishna, Hare Krishna, Krishna Krishna, Hare Hare
Hare Rama, Hare Rama, Rama Rama, Hare Hare

Table of Contents

Chapter 1 Introduction to Hinduism 5

Chapter 2 Hindu Philosophy 9

Chapter 3 Concept of Maya in Hinduism 15

Chapter 4 What is Karma? 18

Chapter 5 Soul (Aatma) in Hinduism 22

Chapter 6 Reincarnation in Hinduism 26

Chapter 7 Brahman - The Supreme Being 30

Chapter 8 Why Hindus Worship Idols? 34

Chapter 9 Mantras in the Hindu Religion 37

Chapter 10 Practice of Yoga in Hinduism 41

Chapter 11 Vegetarianism in the Hindu Religion 45

Chapter 12 The Caste System in the Hindu Religion 49

Chapter 13 Popular Hindu Gods and Goddesses 53

Chapter 14 Symbolism of Arms in Hindu Gods and Goddesses 64

Chapter 15 Hindu Swastika 68

Chapter 16 The Aum 71

Chapter 17 Holy books of the Hindus 75

Chapter 18 The Mahabharata 79

Chapter 19 Bhagavad Gita 82

Chapter 20 The Ramayana 89

Chapter 21 River Ganges in the Hindu religion 95

Chapter 22 The cow in Hindu religion 99

Chapter 23 Major Hindu Festivals 102

Chapter 24 Important Hindu Holy places to visit in India 108

Chapter 25 Tips for visiting a Hindu temple 113

Chapter 26 Conclusion 118

Chapter 1
Introduction to Hinduism

Hinduism is an ancient religion that goes back to prehistoric times. It is the third most widely followed religion in the entire world and has over 750 million followers, with most of them residing in India. The followers of Hinduism are called Hindus. The Hindu name comes from an Indian river called the Indus River. According to archaeologists and researchers, Hinduism may have started as long ago as 2000 B.C. That would make it a 4000 year old religion, which means it is the oldest religion in the world. In modern times, India has more than 80% of its population that still follows the Hindu faith. Since the population of India is close to 1.3 billion people, this is a considerable percentage of the population that follows Hinduism. Over the years there have been other Hindu followers outside of India, but most of them were merely immigrants that came from India or had family members who subjected them to the Hindu teachings in some form. But India still holds the record for the most Hindu followers in one country.

Lord Krishna

Hinduism is a unique religion because it does not have a founder or a prophet that started the faith. This is unusual for an old religion because most religions from ancient times had to rely on prophets to keep spreading the words of their faith throughout the years. Instead, Hinduism became a collection of different religious beliefs all rolled into one. Then around 1500 B.C., this collection of beliefs were written down in Sanskrit and compiled into a holy book called "Vedas." This is considered to be the oldest holy book in the world. In fact, it was written over a thousand years before the Holy Bible even existed. The Vedas is used to teach people how they should live their daily lives and how to help their families and friends maintain their faith. But as the Vedas writings have been reinterpreted and rewritten countless times over the centuries, the belief system and Hindu way of thinking has also changed right along with it. The only thing that followers seem to have in common is their belief in the one universal God, who is called "Brahman." Brahman does not have one physical appearance or interpretation though. Brahman exists in many different forms, so it is impossible to interpret this God in just one way. Hindus believe that everyone has a part of Brahman inside of them. Not only that, but Brahman guides all people in their lives. In order for people to realize this, Brahman takes on the form of many smaller gods and helps people find their way to understanding what the main god truly is.

The Vishnupad Temple in the Indian state of Bihar, India.

When Hindus pray they are actually praying to their personal god or goddess, which represent different forms of Brahman. Hindus believe these gods are sent to Earth to help people find Brahman in their lives and eventually connect their soul to the universal soul of

Brahman in the afterlife. Some of the personal gods that Hindus commonly pray to are Brahma, Vishnu, Shiva, Saraswathi, Parvati, Hanuman, Krishna, Rama and Ganesha. Each of these Gods represents something different about the world. For example, Brahma is the creator of the universe. His goddess wife, Saraswati, is the goddess of wisdom. She represents knowledge and creativity in the world. Shiva is known as the destroyer because he is responsible for the dissolution and recreation of life in the universe. But even though all of these gods may represent something different, they are all part of Brahman. Therefore, it doesn't really matter which god a Hindu chooses to believe in because they all represent life in some fashion.

Chapter 2
Hindu Philosophy

Hindu philosophy is quite difficult to understand and the traditions and beliefs surrounding Hinduism may vary between various schools of thought. The concepts written in the Vedas are generally what are preached to Hindus or those learning about it. However, there are other schools and teachings of Hinduism that don't use the Vedas as their main source for teaching its traditions. Instead they develop their own traditions based on ideas and concepts from things that are not spiritual based. There are two Indian names that differentiate these teachings. The "astika" or orthodox teachings are the ones that rely on the Vedic literature as the source of their religious beliefs. The opposite name "nastika" or "not astika" are the non-orthodox philosophies. In other words, the nastika teaching system does not use any of the Vedic literature. The traditions of nastika are simply derived from mere thought.

The six astika schools of thoughts include:

1. **Yoga** is about meditation, contemplation and liberation so that the soul can connect with the Supreme Being.

2. **Samkhya** is one of the six orthodox schools of thought. This philosophy classifies the world into realities namely the "Purusa" (the consciousness) and "Prakriti" (the matter). The living is bounded to the Purusa and Prakriti. Letting go of ego and spiritual awakening is very important in the Samkhya philosophy.

3. **Nyaya philosophy** is about the use of logic and exploring knowledge. It states that human suffering is due to humans engaging in wrong doings because of wrong knowledge. One can overcome this by acquiring right knowledge particularly about the soul, the self and the reality.

4. **Vaisheshika philosophy** is type of naturalism that states that everything is reduced to atoms and liberation can be achieved by understanding the world. All experiences of people are derived from the interplay of substances.

5. **Mimamsa** means "investigation, inquiry, discussion" in Sanskrit. This philosophy looks at the interpretation of the Vedas, the earliest scriptures of Hinduism and other Hindu texts. The main role of this philosophy is to enlighten Dharma and provide justification of the rituals. It can be considered as an intellectual force behind Hinduism and formation of Hindu law.

Adi Shankara, 800 C.E., is supposed to be one of the most respected philosophers of India. He travelled throughout India to propagate his views.

6. **Vedanta** actually means knowledge and the end of the Veda. It is concerned with the interpretation of the Hindu texts particularly the Upanishads, the Brahma Sutras and the Bhagavad Gita.

The nastika schools of thought include:

Carvaka is one of the heterodox or atheistic schools of thought that stresses on materialism.

Ajivika is another of the heterodox school of thought linked to a group of wandering ascetics.

Both the heterodox (unorthodox) school of thoughts became extinct over time. It is thought that the Jain and Buddhist traditions sprang from the heterodox movements which became separate religions.

Goals of life - **Dharma, Artha, Kama and Moksha**

Hindus basically have four goals that they try to achieve in their lifetime. These goals are described as Dharma, Artha, Kama (not be confused with Karma) and Moksha.

The goal of **Dharma** simply means doing one's duty. It's a standard by which people should live. For instance, Dharma also means being kind to your parents and elders. Hindus believe this kindness will guide people to a better life. They also believe that a son who gets married is showing respect to their parents so this is the son's dharma. Doing bad deeds is going against dharma.

Artha is a goal that many people throughout the world have, even those who are not Hindu. It means working hard to generate wealth and a stable living for yourself and your family. The only stipulation is that it has to be achieved through lawful means.

Kama is about fulfilling desires. Desires can be in many forms; from wealth, sexual needs, spiritual or doing something one really wants etc. The world kama is often linked with sex as in Kama Sutra but has broader meanings. It also means affection, love, desires, and wishes without the sexual associations.

Moksha is a goal for being good to other people by showing them kindness and doing favors for them. Sometimes it is hard for people to show kindness, especially to those who are not kind in return. But through yoga exercises and mediation, Hindus are able to clear out their negative feelings and resentments. It is said that people who follow this path will eventually have their souls released from the cycle of rebirth and be united with the universal soul, Brahman. This is what all Hindus are trying to achieve. The achievement of Moksha goes much deeper than simply being nice to others though. Hindus can choose one of four paths to take in order to achieve Moksha and unite their soul with Brahman. Doing good deeds and showing kindness to others is just one path. The three other paths are of knowledge, meditation and devotion. The path of knowledge means you have spiritual knowledge about the relationship between your soul and the universal soul of Brahman. The path of meditation is where you meditate to become one with Brahman by finding your real self inside of you. As for the path of devotion, this involves choosing a god to worship throughout your life. This devotion means you speak their words and act the way they want you to act. Of course, Hindus can choose multiple paths if they want to increase their chances of achieving Moksha. But they must choose at least one path to have a chance at it.

Karma

Then finally a word about, Karma is a special goal that most people are familiar with. Hindus believe that if you do good things for others, then good things will happen to you in return. This is due to your karma. However, if you do bad things then bad things will happen to you as well. In most cultures, people pass around the word "Karma" with this exact same meaning. But little do they realize that it comes from the Hindu faith. The Hindus believe that reincarnation of the soul is determined by karma. Since Hindus are trying to achieve Moksha in their life, this gives them more of an incentive to keep their karma strong by doing good deeds. That way their soul can join the universal god Brahman after they die.

Chapter 3
Concept of Maya in Hinduism

Maya is a word that means "magic" or "illusion." Hindus interpret the definition in a lot of different ways, and over the centuries it has had multiple meanings. Before the Vedic texts were written, Maya was construed as merely an absolute wisdom and power that one possesses. But then after the Vedic texts were compiled and written, Maya took on a different meaning. It was thought of as an illusion of what we see around us. This meant that what we see in the present may not be real or what it appears to be. The Vedic texts use the Indian traditions and philosophies to describe Maya. It stated that everything which exists is constantly changing all the time and the only spiritual reality is the force that hides a person's true character. This force creates the illusion you now know as Maya. Hindus spend their whole lives trying to break free of this illusion by studying the Vedic texts and understanding how perfect our inner souls actually are.

A Shiv ling (or lingam) is a symbol of energy representing Lord Shiva.

In the Vedanta philosophies of Hinduism, it teaches that our true nature is perfect and totally divine. We don't have to pray to Brahman (Supreme Being) for help or guidance in our lives. Brahman is a part of all of us, including our inner soul known as Atman. Therefore, how can nature be anything but perfect if we all have Brahman inside of us? People often wonder why they don't have this divine awareness about Brahman. Instead they think the nature of the world is imperfect, which makes it hard for them to follow this faith. However, the Hindu teachings explain that Maya is the reason for their ignorance. Maya is like a giant sheet that covers up the true state of nature and the world around us. Nobody can explain why Maya exists. We just know that it is there. But what we do know is that Maya does not exist once we have knowledge of our true nature. We get this by gaining wisdom about ourselves and the world. We have to realize that Brahman exists inside of everything and everyone.

So, how does someone gain this wisdom when the world appears to be so evil and godless? The answer goes back to karma. You have to do good deeds by being kind and generous to others. It is through good deeds where one can help develop wisdom and knowledge about the part of Brahman inside of them. Once this discovery is made, Maya cannot cover it any longer. But, you have to do more than just good deeds to get this knowledge. You have to study the philosophies of Hinduism and understand all of this through the Hindu teachings. Maya is a hard concept to understand for those outside of the Hindu faith. Laypeople look at the world and see nothing but war, disease, death and old age. They also feel hatred, anger and many other emotional miseries and wonder why these feelings exist if nature is supposed to be so perfect. Since these negative feelings affect the body and mind, many would say these are the two main aspects of life. Therefore, nature must be imperfect. But what they have to realize is that all this physical and emotional suffering does not impact the one true thing that makes up our real nature, which is Atman. Maya tries to make people ignorant to the fact that Atman even exists, which is why there is so much skepticism outside of the Hindu faith. But once you understand Maya and discover Atman for yourself, you will realize how perfect our inner soul truly is. This perfection comes from Brahman being a part of all of us.

Chapter 4
What is Karma?

Karma is a word that describes the type of action one takes and the results of that action. In other words, every action has a reaction. The word "karma" comes from an Indo-European word that means "to do." Hindus believe that karma is what governs all of our lives. Modern day people often confuse the meaning of karma by associating it with fate. They think every action you take will inflict an equal type of action upon you. The truth is that karma refers to all of the actions in our lives, not just a select few. If you live a life of kindness and generosity towards others then your next life may be filled with less pain and hardship. But if you are bad to others then you may be reborn into a worse life. This is really the gist of how Hindus think of karma and so they try to live their lives to sustain a positive karma.

Havan: Fire or Agni is also considered as a God in Hinduism. Agni plays an important role in Hindu traditions and religious rituals particularly during offerings, cremations and weddings. It is thought that anything offered to Agni will be taken to the Gods.

Karma is known in both Hinduism and Buddhism. Although the meanings in both religions are generally the same, there is a slight difference in the interpretation. Hindus believe that karma is actually given to you by the gods, especially Brahman. On the other hand, Buddhists do not believe in any gods. They just believe that karma happens naturally to all of us. Hindus look at karma as a law, which is why it is generally referred to as the law of karma. This law states that all life on earth is controlled by cause and effect, or action and reaction. This is how somebody's deeds or actions will affect their future in the next life. For example, if you know somebody who has suffered great misfortune in their life and has never done anything bad, they are likely experiencing this misfortune because of the wrongful actions they made in a previous life. This is how Hindus interpret karma.

Karma was first mentioned in the ancient Hindu texts known as "Rig Veda," which is one of the oldest Vedic Sanskrit to ever be found. However, the Rig Veda just describes karma as a simple religious action, such as an animal sacrifice. It wasn't until later when other Vedic Sanskrit texts were written in 600 B.C. that karma was perceived as a cause and effect based upon a person's actions. This collection of texts is called Upanishads. Ever since this text was written, this is what Hindus have followed in their traditions in terms of karma and its law of nature that gods do not interfere with people's actions. We just have to obtain the knowledge of karma and realize our course of actions have to be good in order to receive good karma.

Many Hindus believe there is both good karma and bad karma. The more good actions you conduct in your life, the more it will get rid of any negative effects caused by bad karma. The whole purpose of life is to get rid of bad karma as much as possible. This is how you will have the best chance of having a better life when you get reincarnated after death. There are two schools of thought that believe there are three different types of karma. These schools are primarily from the Vedanta and Yoga teachings of Hinduism. They teach that there is "Prarabdha karma", "Sanchita karma", and "Kriyamana karma". Prarabdha is when you experience past karmas in the present. Sanchita is the collection of these past experiences that lead you to prarabdha. Then finally, Kriyamana is how our present actions will affect our future lives. Basically, it's the all the karma humans produce in their entire life. The ideas are the same, but these philosophies break karma down into these three groups to further explain the various stages of karma.

Chapter 5
Soul (Aatma) in Hinduism

Aatma, also referred to as **Atman**, is a word that comes from Sanskirt and means "soul." Hindus believe Atman is their inner-self, or true self, and this represents their soul. Hinduism is the first major Indian religion to describe and believe in an eternal soul. If you look at the other popular Indian religion, Buddhism, it does not subscribe to the belief of any eternal soul. Hinduism schools teach that we all have an eternal self, which is the lord of our bodies. The body gives enjoyment to the soul, but does not represent the soul. All living beings in this world, including insects, animals and plants, have atman inside of them. Atman is the sole reason life exists in the first place. If there were no Atman, then all life in the Cosmos would be motionless matter.

Hindu cremation on the banks of the River Ganges in the holy city of Varanasi. The ultimate aim of the Hindus is to attain Moksha or become free from the recycle of birth.

When a physical being is about to be born, the soul within the body activates it. This soul is what gets the heart pumping blood and the lungs breathing air. Then after the big bang occurred in the Cosmos, the Atman was created and they journeyed across the universe to find planets that were hospitable. Earth was one of these planets where the Atman settled. Eventually the environments on Earth began to change to a point where life could be sustained. Mother Earth needs to allow life to be sustained before Atman can help form a new being. So basically, Mother Earth and Atman work together to create new life on the planet. Then as beings get born and die, the Atman keeps getting recycled to form new life with the same soul. After millions of manifestations, the soul will reach its peak for regenerating new life. This is when an enlightened being will be born.

The stage of "**moksha**" is what Hindus are most excited about. This is the stage where the atman leaves the body forever, and the cycle of birth and death finally stops. This means the atman will never inhabit another body ever again. Once a person's soul has gained moksha, they will live within the kingdom of God. This kingdom is known by Hindus as Vaikuntha (heaven). It is a world full of aatmas where no physical beings or bodies exist. All the souls in this kingdom had manifested themselves into bodies approximately 8.4 million times and have traveled for about 96 million years. It is through all of these body manifestations that the soul becomes pure and cleansed, which means it does not need to manifest itself again. Then as Atman enters the kingdom of God, it will be amongst all the other cleansed souls with no chance of being impure ever again.

While Hindus continue on their journey towards moksha, they want to make each new life as wonderful as possible. This is where karma comes into the picture. They try to do good deeds in order to receive a positive reaction, which is a better life after they are reborn. Since atman takes a long time before it gets moksha, the lives we are born into need to be as comfortable as possible. Otherwise, it will be a longer and tougher road to the kingdom of Vaikuntha. If you want to learn more about how Atman manifests itself inside a body until it reaches enlightenment, this information can be found in the Hindu Doctrine of Bhagavad Gita. Hindus believe that in order to gain enlightenment, you have to understand all of the verses, or shloka, that are in the Bhagavad Gita. By gaining this newfound knowledge, the atman cycle of life can finally be complete.

Chapter 6
Reincarnation in Hinduism

Reincarnation is a very active belief in the Hindu religion. Hinduism teaches that when a person dies, their soul enters a new body and they get reborn again. The quality of their new life usually has to do with the karma of their previous life. Karma simply means an "act" or "deed" that one partakes in. For every action you take, whether good or bad, you will have a reaction. This is the cause and effect principle that is highly believed by people of the Hindu faith. So if you commit evil acts in your life, then you will eventually be reincarnated into a new life where you will have evil acts done to you. On the flip side, if you do positive deeds and help others then you will be reincarnated into a better life. Not only that, but you will keep getting closer to reaching enlightenment. Once you get to this point, the reincarnation cycle will stop and your soul will live in the Kingdom of God for all eternity.

The soul of a person can travel from one being to another till it reaches perfection and attains moksha.

Samsara is the Hindu word that describes the cycle of life and death caused by reincarnation. Hindus believe the law of karma is primarily to control samsara. The more life and death the soul experiences, the more karma that is being generated for that soul. Good actions cause good karma to be accumulated and bad actions cause bad karma to be accumulated. As you keep building up one of these types of karma, you take it with you to the next life. If you realize that you have bad karma, for example, then you can still change your ways and perform better actions in order to save your soul from more bad karma. Remember that karma is not controlled or managed by any God. Instead it is something that individuals have control over themselves. So whatever they did in their present life, the karma they built up will travel with their soul and get reborn with them in their next life.

The Hindu word that describes the liberation from samsara is "moksha." This is the final goal that a Hindu will achieve with their soul. The first three goals are artha, kama and dharma. These goals represent the extra benefits you will get after being reincarnated with good karma. You will endure pleasure, virtue and power within your samsara. Once these are all achieved, then the soul will find its way to moksha. This is what leads to the Kingdom of God and a chance to be free from all the earthly pain and suffering. But to even have a chance at getting this far, you have to stop deliberately trying to achieve it. A person needs to understand that Brahman is already a part of them and is the universal God. You have to gain this knowledge and give up any desires or pursuits outside of this. This is how you will get moksha.

The whole idea of reincarnation was created by Hindus under the belief that all life on earth came to exist very gradually. In other words, some Hindus don't believe that life just suddenly appeared on earth by a God that created everything. Instead they hold the evolution theory in high regard. It is evolution that allowed people to overcome their imperfections and carry good karma with them to each new life they were born into. As far as modern day societies go, we still have a lot more imperfections that we need to correct. It is true that more people have rights and freedoms around the world, but not everyone. Evolution is still present and we are continuing to gradually evolve as we change our imperfections through reincarnation.

I want to point out that there are 3 types of Vedanta school of thought (or subdivisions of Vedanta Philosophy) on the relationship of the liberated soul with God. They are Dvaita, Advaita and Visishtadvaita. Dvaita is where the soul of the individual is different to the Supreme Being. Once the soul becomes liberated, it gets close to the Supreme Being but does not become part of it. Dvaita also indicates that everything is real. Advaita school of thought says that the world is an illusion. It also says that the soul and God is one and the soul becomes part of God when it achieves moksha. Visishtadvaita is where the Supreme Being is ultimate and has numerous attributes which is different from the individual soul. The goal of the aatman is to reach the "Paramatman" (Supreme Being) in the same way the goal of each drop of water is to reach for the ocean.

Chapter 7
Brahman - The Supreme Being

When you study the ancient Vedic Sanskrit of
Hinduism, you will find there is one thing that is held
on a pedestal as being "absolute." This absolute of
Hinduism represents the ultimate goal of all Hindus.
The Sanskrit language refers to this goal and absolute
as "Brahman" (not to be confused with Brahmin which
is a caste in Hinduism). The word is derived from
another Sanskrit root word "brh," which basically
means "to grow." The root word was commonly used
with brhati, which means "to that which grows," and
brhmayati, which means "which causes to grow." The
true meaning of Brahman is described in a lot of
different ways. In Hinduism, he is usually referred to
as the universal God, or the Supreme Being. However,
his existence goes way beyond just being a God. He is
more of the universal soul that all life on Earth has
inside of them. Every human being, animal, and insect
we see has a bit of Brahman inside of them. You
cannot identify Brahman through just one shape or
form. He takes on many shapes and forms because
Brahman is in everything. That is why there are no
statues or idols that show the true form of Brahman.
Instead there are many different idols that show the
various attributes of Braham and all the other gods
and goddess that are made of him.

Hindus are all searching for the knowledge and
awareness of Brahman in their lives, and throughout
the world. This is a difficult task though because the
human desires for pleasure, money and virtue cause a
distraction from the ultimate reality of Brahman. Have
you ever felt like something was missing in your life?
Perhaps you want more wealth or you want to lose
weight in order to look better and feel better. All of

these desires create restlessness where we keep thinking about these things over and over again. What we don't realize is that we are really trying to find that ultimate reality where our knowledge of Brahman is the only thing that matters. You obtain this knowledge by studying the Hindu scriptures and ancient Sanskrit that outlines all of these rules and traditions.

The concept of Brahman can be hard for some people to understand. Even though he is called a universal god, he is not actually a god in the way you might be thinking. Other religions may think of god as the "old man in the sky" or the Supreme being that watches down over all of us and guides our lives by listening to our prayers. Brahman is not that kind of god. In fact, Brahman cannot even truly be called a "he," because there is no gender associated with him. It is a matter of how you perceive Brahman in your own minds. Some people call him a "he" and others call him an "it." Brahman is really both of these things because his energy resides in men, women, children and material things all around us.

Lord Krishna with Radha. Followers of Krishna believe him to be the Supreme Being.

Brahman is the reason for all reality and the creation of the world. Hindus do not believe the world was creating out of nothing, which is often termed ex nihilo creation. Instead, Hindus believe Brahman is both the efficient cause and the material cause of all creation. It is the main source of dharma and the only true reality in existence. All life we see on Earth did not just get created on its own. It was created from the image of Brahman and all the evolution that has happened since the beginning of time is just a reflection of the transformations and manifestations of Brahman. Then once all life ends on earth, Brahman will have finished manifesting himself throughout the world.

Chapter 8
Why Hindus Worship Idols?

India is one of the few countries in the world where you will see an extensive manufacturing system of idols and people worshipping them. Other cultures may look at idols and just see a doll being worshipped as a godly figure. In Hinduism people do not worship idols because they think it represents God. In fact, Hindus are quite aware that the idols are man-made and created into different shapes. But, what do these shapes mean? If you notice there are many idols that look similar, but have different shapes and attributes. All of these attributes are supposed to be symbolic manifestations of the one Supreme God known as Brahman. Again, it is not an idol that is supposed to be Brahman because he takes on many different shapes and forms. In fact, you will see idols made of the various gods and goddesses of Hinduism. The three gods that are primary manifestations of Brahman are Brahma, Vishnu and Shiva. The creator of life, the sustainer of life and the destroyer of life are all represented by these three gods. Idols are created to capture the attributes of these three gods in order to understand the forces of nature more clearly. By obtaining this understanding and freeing your mind of physical desires, you can actually transform yourself from a physical entity into a divine entity.

A good analogy to idol worshipping is the moon. Between the day of the new moon and full moon, you have 14 nights in between that are all different because the moon takes different shapes. However, it is still the same moon even though it has different impacts on the world. The energy within our bodies can be rearranged differently as well, even though the body is still the same mass of flesh. By rearranging the energies within your body, you are changing yourself into a divine entity. This is why so many Hindus practice yoga in front of idols. At first, yoga might seem like a physical exercise that you perform in order to relax the mind and body from any thoughts and desires. But after awhile it becomes so much more. It becomes a practice where people worship their body because it has become a divine entity.

There are a lot of religions that dismiss idol worshipping as just an act of superstition. Hinduism, on the other hand, takes idol worshipping very seriously. Hindus worship idols as a way to express their love, faith and complete devotion to the world and to become a divine entity. For many, it is also a chance to acquire knowledge and understanding of the one universal god; Brahman. But again, they are not actually worshipping Brahman when they pray in front of an idol. They are worshipping the energy and the many forms of Brahman that make up who we are on this earth.

Idols of Lord Ganesha

To worship an idol, a Hindu will stand in front of it and bow down in complete submission. This means their mind, body and soul all become one with the idol, which allows them to discover Brahman and acquire knowledge about its true existence. In order to get into a place of complete submission, you have to be willing to give up your materialistic ways. Things like money and possessions have to be far from your mind because they are just a distraction from the true nature of the universe. But once you are finally realizing the truth, you will acknowledge the presence of God and be just one step closer from reaching the enlightened path. This is the place all where Hindus want to be after their cycle of life has ended.

Chapter 9
Mantras in the Hindu Religion

Mantra is considered to be a sacred sound that usually comes in the form of a word, syllable, phrase, prayer or hymn. Mantras have been used for thousands of years and the tradition surrounding its use still exists. The words used to make the sounds come from Sanskrit. The reason for Mantra varies between the different Hindu schools that teach it. Mantra may be used as a magical chant or through a spiritual medium with the supernatural forces of nature. The whole purpose of performing these sounds or chants is to receive some kind of mental or physical benefit from these forces. Mantra is just a way to connect them to our own lives. Some Hindus believe Mantra is a communication link to the Gods which allows them to ask for protection against something bad. Sometimes they'll even ask to help someone else through the mantras. But overall, Hindus will ask for support in their own lives. This could be support for wealth, fame, peace of mind, or even to conceive a child. In a way, they are basically praying to their higher power to grant them these wishes or desires. It is the same way Catholic people pray to their God for help when they need it. The only difference is Hindus aren't praying to just one God. There are multiple gods in Hinduism and they all serve a different purpose. It is up to the worshipper to decide which God they want to pray to and what they want to ask them.

ॐ भूर्भुवः स्वः
तत्सवितुर्वरेण्यं
भर्गो देवस्य धीमहि
धियो यो नः प्रचोदयात्

The Gayatri Mantra: One of the most revered mantra of the Vedic tradition.

Mantra is a word that comes from ancient Sanskrit text. Its root word "Man" means the mind and its suffix "tra" means a tool. So when you put them together you get "mind tool" has a translation to the complete word. The mind tool that mantra refers to is the tool of using your voice to produce sound. The secret to performing mantra is in the pronunciation of the word you are chanting. Even though you are repeating the same word or phrase over and over again, it is important that you keep saying it correctly or else it won't serve its purpose. The whole concept behind mantra is to help you concentrate more when you mediate. The idea is that if you keep hearing the exact same sound over and over again, it will relax your mind and block out all other sounds or distractions. It is similar to how modern day people listen to white noise because it contains consistent sound waves that never change frequencies. Mantra is actually an early form of white noise because people chant the same word to themselves without ever saying another word.

Mantra is not exclusive to just Hinduism nor did it originate from it. There are other religions that conduct mantras, such as Buddhism, Sikhism and Jainism. However, their interpretation of mantra and its powers are different. With Buddhism, for example, the Buddhists believe that the mantra sounds actually have supernatural powers. These powers are supposed to help people perform better in their lives and rid themselves of negative thoughts. In Hinduism, followers would say that Gods are the "supernatural forces" helping you. Buddhists don't have any Gods, so they just call them spirits. But the concepts are basically still the same. Hinduism is the religion that uses mantra the most though. It has become a regular tradition amongst its followers that is still being used thousands of years after it was created. The most popular word that is chanted is "Om." The sound of this pronunciation is said to be the first sound ever created in the universe. It is the sound that represents life, death and the cycle of birth. This is the sound that will help Hindus reach enlightenment.

Many Hindus would recite a mantra in their mind on the go while some would use a 108 bead rosary called a "mala" to help them recite and count the number of times the mantras have been chanted.

Here are some of the popular Hindu mantras:

The Gayatri Mantra: One of the most popular mantras for purification and healing purposes.

Om Bhur Bhuvah Svah, Tat-Savitur Varenyam

Bhargo Devasya Dhimahi, Dhiyo Yo Nah Pracodayat

Maha Mrityunjaya Mantra: The mantra dedicated to Lord Shiva. It is supposed to purify the karmas of the soul and help elongate life.

*Om Tryambakam Yajamahe, Sugandhim
Pushtivardhanam
Urvarukamiva Bandhanan, Mrityor Mokshiya Mamritat*

ॐ त्र्यम्बकं यजामहे सुगन्धिंम् पुष्टिवर्धनम्
उर्वारुकमिव बन्धनान् मृत्योर्मुक्षीय मामृतात्

The Mahamrityunjaya Mantra

Ganesha Mantra: A mantra dedicated to Lord Ganesha. Its objective is to remove obstacles.

Om Gam Ganapataye Namaha

Hanuman Mantra: The mantra dedicated to Lord Hanuman (the monkey God).

Om Shri Hanumate Namaha

The **Maha Mantra** dedicated to Lord Vishnu (Rama and Krishna were incarnations of Vishnu).

*Hare Krishna Hare Krishna, Krishna Krishna Hare Hare
Hare Rama Hare Rama, Rama Rama Hare Hare*

Chapter 10
Practice of Yoga in Hinduism

Yoga is a word that comes from the Sanskrit word "yuj," which means "to yoke." This represents the union of the souls with the universal soul of Brahman. It is where your mind, body and soul become one with Brahman. The, of course, over the centuries this meaning had been changed countless times by yoga practitioners who strived away from the original Sanskrit meaning. Now yoga has been transformed into a variety of practices that are conducted by people from all walks of life.

Kapalbhati pranayam on the beach in Goa.

Most people in the world have heard of yoga. But outside of religion, people often perceive it as just a bunch of physical exercises where you twist your body into weird positions. In the United States, for example, people take up yoga as a form of physical exercise.

But to Hindus, it has a much bigger meaning entirely. In fact, the true historical significance of yoga comes from Hinduism. The ancient Hindus of India created yoga as a form of spiritual practices that help people enhance their lives and help them obtain liberation from the recycle of birth. It was through these practices that they were able to let go negative feelings from the physical world, like stress and anxiety. Instead, they could just become a free spirit that could acquire knowledge about the true importance of life and the way they need to live it. People often receive emotional stability, mental clarity, and increased joy in their life after practicing yoga. This ultimately helps them build good karma and gets them on the right path in their cycle of life. Then as they keep bringing their good karma with them into the next life, they will be closer to the path of enlightenment. This is what all Hindus wish to achieve someday with their souls.

The purpose of Yoga still varies amongst Hindus. While some people use it to better themselves, others believe it brings them closer to God. This could be Brahman or one of the many personal Gods or Goddesses that Brahman is a part of. Hindus want to express their love to God by showing them they understand and accept their existence. They feel this will help them keep good karma and will score them extra points in the cycle of rebirth after they die. After all, the ultimate goal of Hindus is to become liberated from the sufferings and pain of the world by obtaining moksha. Some Hindus believe yoga is a ritual that you need to perform in order to achieve this goal and break free of Samsara, which is the word that describes the cycle of birth and death. However, other Hindus think yoga is just a way to help you become a better person, but it isn't required to reach enlightenment.

Yoga is better suitable for people who have preexisting bad karma and want to change their ways by replacing it with good karma. Yoga can certainly help if you have the right practitioner to show you the right way to perform it. The biggest benefit from yoga doesn't come from the physical postures and exercises, but rather from the meditation of the mind. This is how you break free of all your problems and evil thoughts. Meditation through yoga is not just practiced by Hindus either. People of all religions have incorporated this form of yoga into their lives. Atheists and nonbelievers have even taken part in yoga, despite its origins coming from religion in the first place. Some call yoga and meditation mental trickery while others call it a gift from the Gods to help you perform good deeds. Either way the practice of yoga works and is one of the most popular rituals of the Hindu faith. There is no doubt that here are numerous health benefits of yoga too. For instance, it helps increase flexibility and improves posture, builds strength, protects the spine, increases blood flow, facilitates breathing and so on.

Here are some yoga techniques that you wish to explore.

Kapalbhati Pranayam is a breathing exercise that is very popular in India. It is done by sitting on the ground in a typical yoga posture (crossed leg and straight spine) and inhaling normally and exhaling forcibly. Basically, the idea is to inhale deeply (normally) and exhaling quickly for up to 10 breaths. When you inhale, your tummy should go "outwards" and while exhaling forcibly, the tummy should go "inwards". It is supposed to help cranial sinuses and also helps obtain a flat tummy.

Cobra or the also known as the "**Bhujanga Asana**" is another easy one you can try. Lie flat on your tummy and place your chin on the floor and feet together. Place you hands near the chest with palms down on floor and elbows raised. When inhaling, curl your torso of the floor as far as possible while pressing the hip region on the floor. Breathe naturally. Then exhale while releasing the torso back to the floor. This asana strengthens the muscles of the shoulders, neck and back. It is also supposed to help asthma patients. But those suffering from diseases of the gastrointestinal tract should not do it.

Pawan Mukt Asana is supposed to release any trapped gas in the large intestine. But do not do this if you suffer from any abdominal issues, hernia or piles. Life flat on the floor; fold your right leg up at the knee while inhaling and hold it with your hand locked together. Then raise your upper part of the body and touch the raised right knee with your nose. Hold it at this position as long as you can. Then release the leg and place it back where it was while exhaling. Then repeat this with your left leg. Remember to inhale when raising the leg and exhaling when releasing the leg.

Chapter 11
Vegetarianism in the Hindu Religion

Many Hindus around the world, especially in India, have made vegetarianism an integral part of their daily life. It is actually a tradition and spiritual practice because Hindus have to practice being non-violent in every possible way. This means their speech, thoughts, and actions have to reflect someone who is nonviolent in nature. For some Hindus, this can be hard to do. The Hindu schools teach people about vegetarianism, but it really comes down to a choice in the end. This is because vegetarianism is not actually a requirement under the old Hindu teachings. According to the Manusmriti, it is not a sin to eat meat. However, you will receive great rewards if you are able to refrain from eating it. So if you think that you will have to become a vegetarian if you become a Hindu, don't worry because you won't. In fact only 30% of the Hindu population is actually vegetarian. The rest of them eat meat.

A plate of vegetarian food offered during a Hindu ceremony. The plate has a couple of puris, mater-paneer, a potato curry, a gulab jamun, some salad along with rice and raita.

The main reason there are vegetarians in Hinduism has to do with nonviolence towards animals. As you know, Hindus are constantly worrying about their karma. They want to make sure they build up enough good karma so they can take it with them into the next life after they die. One of the rules of getting good karma is to do good deeds and act kindly towards others. This does not just mean human beings though. All life on earth is equally important because it all contains a part of Brahman. Therefore, people are afraid if they kill animals or even eat their meat, it will have negative karmic influences that they will pay for in the next life. The philosophies on the subject vary amongst the different schools of

Hinduism. It is really a matter of what you personally believe and how much of a chance you want to take to generate good karma versus bad karma.

Large number of Hindus prefers to eat vegetarian food.

The ancient Vedic Sanskrit did not ban people from eating meat, but rather they set specific rules and restrictions upon it. For example, people were not allowed to just hunt down an animal and kill it for food. But they were allowed to perform ritual sacrifices on animals, which would ultimately lead to their death. Once the sacrifices were made, the meat of the animal was consumed. Over time, the traditions were slightly altered when it came to eating meat. Now Hindus who want to eat meat are taught to eat meat from an animal that has been killed humanely. There is a process of killing animals called "Jhatka" which means that an animal has been killed quickly. This type of meat comes from an animal that was killed from a single blow or attack. For example, if you take an axe and swing a lethal blow to the animal's head, then the meat of the animal is jhatka. The idea here is the animal has not suffered, so there is no bad karma from killing an animal that wasn't made to suffer first. In other religions, like Islam and Judaism, animals are often killed slowly with ritualistic methods. Hindus would believe this creates bad karma.

The closest that vegetarian Hindus will get to eating meat is consuming milk and dairy products. This would actually make them lacto-vegetarians. Of course, not all Hindus are lacto-vegetarians. Some of them refrain from eating food generated from any part of the animal because they believe it will only increase their good karma even more. As for animal sacrifices, they are still held today. Normally the rituals are formed to honor one of the Hindu Gods. In Nepal, Hindus there honor the Goddess Gadhimai by slaughtering 250,000 animals every five years as a sacrifice to her. Then the meat is consumed as a way to honor her.

In the North of India, wheat is very popular in the form of chapattis, Nan breads, parathas, puris (fried) and eaten manly with vegetable curries. Rice dishes include plain boiled rice, pulau rice and vegetable biryanis. South Indian food is similar but has more rice dishes and curries are spicier.

Chapter 12
The Caste System in the Hindu Religion

The Hindus established a caste system (Varna) in order to keep social order amongst their people. This system was created around 2,000 B.C., which is around the time Hinduism first came into existence. Hindus believe that people have different personalities and characteristics which make them socially different from one another. This means they need to be put into separate groups where they will fit better throughout different aspects of society. There are four primary social groups called "Varnas" that make up these social classes; Brahmin, Kshatriyas, Vaisyas, and Shudras.

A Brahmin priest in a temple

Brahmin (not to be confused with the word *Brahman*, the Supreme Being) is a caste supposed to be made up of spiritual leaders, also known as the reflective ones. This group consists of priests, seers, and reflective individuals. These people perform rituals and study the Vedas and other Sanskrit texts on the Hindu faith. They are the middle men between the gods and people. Remember that Hinduism has multiple Gods, so followers and priests tend to worship more than one God. Many Brahmins are temple priests who will pray to any of the Gods on another's behalf. Brahmins are supposed to spend their lives trying to acquire divine knowledge of the Hindu traditions and then preserve them so that others can learn as well.

Kshatriyas are the warrior class. They are the ones who protect others in society by making sure no harm comes to them. In our present day, we recognize these people as policemen, firefighters, military personnel, and politicians. But the ancient Hindus referred to them as Rajahs (kings), nobles and warriors. Besides protection, they offer sacrifices to the Gods and the spirits of their ancestors. They also study the Vedas and provide gifts to all the Brahmins that help them understand their faith.

The **Vaishyas** are the merchant class. These are the people who manufacture, produce and sell physical goods to others throughout society. They do all kinds of commercial activities such as cultivating land, tending to cattle, lending money and trading goods. And like other classes, the Vedic Sanskrit is thoroughly studied by them. Vaishya can even participate in some Vedic rituals; however, they are forbidden from marrying any woman who is of a higher caste than they are.

Vaishyas are considered as the merchant class for instance this shopkeeper.

The **Shudras** are the working class, or the labor class. In the olden days, they served the Brahmins, Vaisyas, and Kshatriyas with whatever they needed doing. They did menial jobs such as cleaning the toilets, tilling the land, working as laborers etc. Shudras were the one class that were not allowed to study any of the Sanskrit texts or the rituals that came out of it. In fact, they were even restricted from hearing any of the sacred chants that came from the temples. In the 6th century India, discrimination against Shudras was so rife that when they eat food, they could not eat with anyone from the upper three castes nor could they marry any women from other castes either. In addition, they had to live on the outskirts of the towns and villages and enter only to work. They simply had to work hard and make everyone else's lives more manageable. They were even regarded as untouchables.

The caste system falls under what is called the laws of Manu, which describes in Sanskrit what traditions of the caste system that people must obey. Those who did not obey would be punished. Since the ruling class was made of politicians and warriors from the Kshatriyas class, these were the ones who enforced the traditions onto people. This is very similar to our modern day system of politicians and policemen. The politicians make the laws and the policemen enforce them. But with the caste system, the politicians didn't write the traditions. They were just the ones who oversaw its enforcement and the warriors physically carried it out. They saw themselves as the servants of dharma. This caused all other Hindus to abide by the caste system out of fear and superstition.

A word of note here! Caste system has now become less relevant in modern India but it exists. Discrimination against any caste is now a punishable offence by law and practice of untouchability is unacceptable. In the olden days, some sections of society particularly the Shudras were discriminated but now everyone is considered equal in the eyes of the law.

Chapter 13
Popular Hindu Gods and Goddesses

Hinduism is described as complex system of thoughts and beliefs. Some describe Hinduism as monotheistic with Brahman as the Supreme Being with other Gods as its manifestations. Some have described Hinduism as polytheism, pantheism, henotheism, monism where concept of God is difficult to understand. But in essence when Hindus worship one personal God known as "Ishvara", they accept the existence of other Gods. "Trimurti" is another concept in Hinduism where there is a creator (Lord Brahma), the preserver (Lord Vishnu) and the destroyer (Lord Shiva).

Let's take a look at some of Hinduism's polytheistic canon of deities:

Lord Brahma is the creator of the universe and part of the Trimurti. Brahma should not be confused with **Brahman**. It is thought that Brahma was created by Vishnu from his own body that then later created the universe.

Lord Vishnu is known as the peace loving god and the preserver of all life on earth. Vishnu enforces the traits of truth, righteousness and order upon all life in order to minimize hate and deception. If there is ever a time where these values are under attack or being threatened in any way, Vishnu will emerge on earth to restore love and peace in the world. The unique thing about Vishnu is that when he comes to earth in a physical form he has 10 avatars that he lives under. These avatars are the Matsya, Kurma, Varaha, Narasimha, Vamana, Parashurama, Rama, Krishna, Buddha and Kalki (avatar yet to come). In some ancient texts, it is said that Buddha is also an avatar of Vishnu.

Statue of Lord Vishnu

Lord Shiva is the most powerful God, which earned him the nickname of "destroyer." He is also considered to be a more complex God. That is why shrines of Shiva are often in temples that are separate to the shrines of other Gods. Shiva actually represents the energy necessary to sustain life on both macrocosmic and microcosmic levels. In other words, Shiva is the energy that flows through the Earth and throughout the entire universe. But as the destroyer God, his job is to destroy every world in the universe at the end of their creation. They will all be dissolved into complete nothingness. Even scientists have theorized that a black hole will probably wipe out all physical existence in the universe in another billion years. Hindus would say the black hole was really Shiva's doing.

Lord Shiva

Lord Ganesha is known as the Lord of Success, and son of Parvati and Shiva. He is one of the most recognizable Gods in Hinduism. The drawings of him show a floating figure with an elephant head, big ears, pot belly and a mouse next to him. The elephant head is a symbol for the soul, or the Atman, which is the supreme reason for our physical existence. As for Ganesha's body, this symbolizes Maya. Since he is the lord of success, this also makes him the destroyer of all obstacles and evils. Hindus also consider Ganesha to be the God of wisdom, knowledge, education and wealth. It all depends on what "success" means to each individual who prays to Ganesha.

Lord Ganesha with his elephant head

Lord Krishna is a very popular God, and also the eighth incarnation of Vishnu. He is commonly referred to as the God of love and joy. Hindus worship him because he destroys all sin and hardship that comes to us in life. Krishna is also big on education and knowledge, but more importantly he is big on love. He came to earth after all the sins committed by the evil rulers and kings of the time. Brahma prayed to Vishnu to get reborn on earth and destroy the evil that has taken over on it. One of these evils was demon "Narakasura", who was the ruler of Northern India and feared by everyone. So when Vishnu was incarnated into Krishna, he killed Narakasura and liberated his people.

Lord Krishna with Radha

Lord Rama is the symbol of virtue and chivalry. More famously, Rama is the main avatar of the supreme protector known as Lord Vishnu and the seventh incarnation of him. Rama is the embodiment of all morality and truth. Texts refer to Lord Rama as having come to earth to get rid of all the evil forces that existed during the time. Hindus and even Indians of other faith refer to Rama as a significant historical figure that was a hero to the people of ancient India. There was an ancient poet, Valmiki, who wrote a Sanskrit poem about Rama (Ramayana) and his exploits. Hindus to this day read the poem and study Rama's exploits as a way to help guide them in their own lives by finding truth and morality.

Lord Hanuman is often referred to as the Monkey God. He is one of the main characters of the Epic Ramayana who helped Lord Ram find Sita and destroy the demon Ravana of the Kingdom of Lanka. Hanuman is considered as the reincarnation of Lord Vishnu. He is particularly known for his valor, courage, selflessness and devotion.

Lord Hanuman from the devotional song, Hanuman Chalisa.

Goddess Kali is considered as the embodiment of Shakti, the force that keeps the universe going. She is shown as complete black with her tongue hanging out and looking extremely violent. In fact, what she is doing is fighting the demonic forces that engulfed the universe. But those who worship her consider her as the divine mother and regard her as the wife of Lord Shiva.

Goddess Kali by Raja Ravi Varma

Goddess Saraswati is the Goddess of education, knowledge, art, music and wisdom. Hindu students worship her so that she can help her pass the exams. She is seen sitting on a white lotus and holding the musical instrument the "veena".

Goddess Saraswati

Goddess Durga is one of the most revered Goddess of the Hindu pantheon. She is seen with ten arms and riding a tiger. She is considered as the divine mother who will protect mankind from evil. Legend has it that she was created by the Gods to destroy the demon Mahishasura, the lord of the demons. She is worshipped as the supreme power "Shakti" and some texts describe her as the greatest Goddess.

Goddess Lakshmi is the Goddess of money, wealth and prosperity. She is the consort of Lord Vishnu and often worshipped together. She is especially worshiped on the Hindu festival of Diwali. Clay lamps are lit outside and inside the homes to direct her to the house. Devotees believe that by doing this she will visit their homes and bless them with prosperity. She is seen standing on a lotus with four hands. Her hands are supposed to present the four goals of life Dharma, Artha, Kama and Moksha.

Chapter 14
Symbolism of Arms in Hindu Gods and Goddesses

When you look at pictures of Hindu Gods and Goddesses, they often appear to have multiple arms coming out of their body. This is a very common way to portray a God, especially when it is constantly fighting off evil cosmic forces. The arms are supposed to represent the immense ability and power that the God possesses. The most common artistic portrayal of a Hindu God is one where they are in human form, but with more than two arms. This is to express the superhuman power of that God. But these artistic portrayals are not only seen with good Gods that want to protect the earth. Demons and other evil forces with superhuman powers are also portrayed with multiple body parts. But with evil figures, they commonly have multiple heads instead of multiple arms. However, there have been good Gods that have been depicted with multiple heads, like Shiva for example. There have been artistic renderings of him with three heads. The central head represents his true character and the other two heads represent his blissful and fierce attributes.

When you see a Hindu illustration of a God with multiple arms, they often have a weapon or symbolic object in their hands. They are also making a gesture with the object or their hands, which could have multiple meanings. If their palms are facing downwards then it is usually a good sign. A worshipper that sees this image will feel safe and then take refuge away from the evils of the world. The God will likely have a raised foot as well, which indicates total liberation from the injustices of the world. If the palm is facing upwards towards the viewer then this is even better. It means the worshipper is protected and does not have to be afraid of anything. Some artists portray this with an open palm with two middle fingers that are bent. This is also an indication of fearlessness. Now in some cases, the gods will be illustrated with their palms clasped together near their chest. This is a symbol of teaching and to turn the Wheel of Dharma.

Statue of Lord Ganesha: You can see that Ganesha has four hands. His raised hands mean that he will protect his devotees. He is blessing his devotees with his right lower hand. His elephant head denotes his enormous wisdom.

Many outside of the Hindu faith have often questioned why arms are used to represent goodness and fearlessness. How come other body parts are not used? For one thing, the hand is often considered to be the universal symbol for dexterity and giving to other people. So when you have multiple hands and arms being represented by a god, this shows them as being overly generous and protecting their followers from evil forces that wish to do them harm. But for symbolic purposes, the arms are often shown to have swords and daggers to ward off evil beasts that prey upon the innocent and helpless.

Some popular examples of Gods with multiple arms are Vishnu and Durga. Vishnu carries a shankha in his upper left hand, which is a conch that communicates love and understanding to his worshippers. In his lower left hand, he carries a mace that symbolizes the energy and power of the world. The upper right hand holds a discus, which represents the idea that Vishnu will use the weapon in order to protect the world from evil. Finally, he carries a lotus flower in his lower right hand to provide grace upon his followers. Vishnu is a clear example of a protector who fights evil and cares for his followers. As for Durga, she is a Goddess with ten arms that holds weapons in all of her hands. The arms depict the 10 directions which simply mean that she will protect her devotees from all directions. You'll see her with a sword, arrow, and trident; amongst others. She is often riding a lion as well. According to the "Shiva Purana" the demon Mahishasura unleashed terror on earth. Lord Vishnu created Durga and all the Gods gave her divine powers and weapons. Durga eventually defeated the demon and brought peace to the world.

Chapter 15
Hindu Swastika

When you hear the word "Swastika," you probably think of the symbol for the Nazi party from Germany that existed in the 1930s and 1940s. What people don't realize is their symbol derived from a Hindu symbol that is thousands of years old. The symbol looks like two equilateral lines crossed together with their legs bent at the ends at 90°. Before the Nazis ruined the nature of this symbol, it was an ancient symbol that had been used by many religions around the world. However, most of the religions that used the symbol were based in India. Hinduism is the best example of this. If you look in the ancient Vedic texts you will find the word "Svasti," which means good fortune or good luck. The word "swastika" was derived from svasti and means the same thing. Of course, if you show this symbol or speak of swastikas to anyone in the western culture then they will think just the opposite because of the whole Nazi Germany era. But with the Hindus of India and around the world, they hold this symbol in high regards to meaning good fortune. In fact they believe putting this symbol on their buildings will bring good luck to anyone inside of it. That is why a Hindu wedding will likely have a swastika banner to wish the new couple good luck.

There are two kinds of swastika symbols; the right-hand swastika and the left-hand swastika. In appearance, this just means the angular lines are facing a different direction. But to the Hindus, these different swastikas represent two different gods. The right-hand swastika is actually one of the many symbols of the god "Vishnu." It is also a symbol that illustrates the sun, and even the Hindu sun God who goes by the name of "Surya." The direction of the arms on the symbol is supposed to represent the direction that the sun takes each day. It starts in the northern hemisphere, and then goes east, south and then west to where it sets. The Native Americans used this symbol to illustrate the same meaning of the sun as well. The swastika is also the symbol of Lord Ganesha and represents his four qualities namely innocence, purity, auspiciousness and finally supreme devotion to the universal mother.

The left-hand swastika is a symbol of the Hindu Goddess known as "Kali." She is the Goddess of death and destruction of evil (she is the fierce aspect of Durga). Some might get terrified of this Goddess, although it is not supposed to be an evil symbol. It is supposed to just reflect the opposite of the other symbol. Since the right-hand swastika means good fortune, the left-hand swastika represents bad fortune. But you won't find too many Hindus using the left-hand swastika. The symbol is more commonly used amongst Buddhists in the Buddhist religion. Buddhists believe that the left-hand swastika means good fortune as well. But they also believe the swastika is a footprint of Buddha and that it contains his mind and spirit. That is why you will find many Buddhists painting the swastika on their chest because they want to be closer to Buddha. Hindus simply keep it as a symbol of good luck. They do not associate it with any one supreme God.

The Swastika and Om often goes hand-in-hand. You can see the Swastika on the left.

Hindus use the right-hand swastika on just about everything. If you look at ancient Hindu paintings and art, you will see the right-hand swastika on almost all of it. In modern times, it is still used and accepted more than ever. You will find it on their jewelry, doorways, cars, clothing, houses, temples and even cakes. So if you are a westerner that visits India and comes across a Hindu wedding, don't freak out when you see the swastika on the outside. It is not some Neo-Nazi rally. It is just a normal Hindu wedding full of love and joy.

Chapter 16
The Aum

The Aum, often spelled as "Om," is a sacred sound that Hindus often chant during their mantra sessions. People like to refer to this as "Aum" because the Om syllable has three sounds to it "a-u-m." In the Sanskrit text, the 'a' and 'u' vowels are combined together to become the 'o.' The reason why this sound is so sacred is because it represents three major triads of the religion. First you have the three worlds of our existence; heaven, atmosphere and earth. You also have the three main gods of Hinduism; Shiva, Vishnu and Brahma. It refers to the creation, preservation and destruction and presents the trinity and the essence of the Vedas. The Aum sound contains the fundamental nature of the entire universe and all that exists within it to hold the universe together. Hindus use Aum in meditation and throughout their normal daily routines.

The Aum

The Aum also has its own symbol, which is considered to be a sacred symbol because it represents the universal god known as Brahman. As you know, Brahman is considered to be the reason for all existence in the first place. But Brahman is also incomprehensible and un-knownable, which means there is no picture or portrait that represents its appearance. The Aum symbol is actually the closest thing to a portrait that indicates Brahman. Hindus describe the symbol as representing both the clear and unclear aspects of God. The sound of Aum is often called "Pranava," which is a Hindu word that means "Cosmic Sound." In other words, they are saying that the sound of Aum is the universal sound that all life on earth makes. The "OM" is the vibration of the Supreme Being. It is a way to be in tune with the world every time Aum comes from your breath.

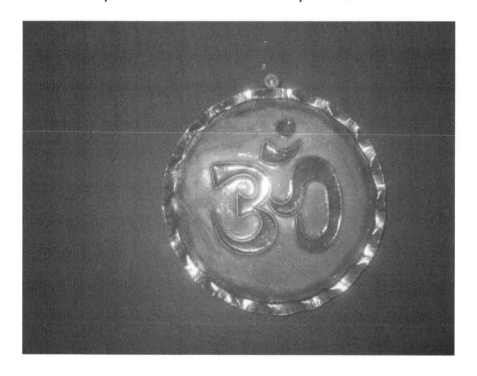

The Aum is often hung on the wall for good luck.

Hindus use Aum every day in their lives. When Hindus wake up in the morning and start their day, they just keep uttering "Aum" as they go about their business. As for the Aum symbol, you will see that in Hindu school and business settings associated with Hinduism. For example, when teachers issue examinations to their students, they will put the Aum symbol at the header of every paper. It is a symbol of spiritual perfection, which would be described by westerners as a good luck charm. That is why some Hindus even wear the symbol as a pendant around their neck. If you go to any Hindu temple or family shrine then you are bound to see this symbol somewhere noticeable. The symbol looks like this: ॐ. If you want to type this symbol on your computer, just choose the Wingdings font and press the backslash key.

Hindus like to mix Aum chants with silence. In between each Aum chant, they take a moment of silence. This causes their mind to move between the silence and the sound until it is able to cease the sound completely. When they are silent they just think about Aum and nothing else. This ultimately puts them into a trance where their physical self comes together with their infinite self, or soul. Once you have reached this stage, all of your worldly problems do not even bother you anymore. All you have is your desire to be one with the universe. This is the power of Aum. Hindus incorporate it into their lives in a variety of ways. If they are at work and are busy then they may hum Aum at their desk or when they go to the bathroom. During their free time, they may practice Aum Yoga which mixes chants in with posture exercises. The point is to integrate it with your free time anyway you can. That is how Hindus try to connect with Brahman as often as they can.

Chapter 17
Holy books of the Hindus

There have been many holy books and ancient Sanskrit texts discovered in the Hindu religion. The main holy books that are studied are the Vedas, Upanishads, Puranas, Ramayana, and the Mahabharata. The oldest of all these religious texts is the Vedas. The word "Veda" can be described as "having knowledge or insight." It is believed by many Hindu scholars that the earliest form of Veda was actually revealed through verbal communication only, around 3000 B.C. This was a time even before Sanskrit was written. In fact, during this era it was prohibited to write down any of the Vedas. Hindus believe the first entity to verbally reveal the Vedas was Brahma, the creator. He only revealed it to certain sages who then passed down the words to other people through speech. You could say these sages were like the prophets of Hinduism, although nobody knows their names or if they really did exist. Eventually the Vedas were written down and retranslated throughout the centuries. It is thought that the Vedas were arranged by a mythical sage called "Veda Vyasa". Some even consider him as an avatar of Lord Vishnu. Hindu scholars refer to the Vedas as Shruti, which means "that which is heard." This goes back to the time when it was only heard. Some of the old school Hindus likes to keep up the early traditions of Vedas by referring to it as a verbal message from Brahman to the world. The shrutis contain much of the history of Hinduism and forms the earliest of the Hindu texts.

If you look at the Vedas you will find many mantras and hymns in written form in the Sanskrit language.

They represent various worldly topics like nature, human behavior, and lifestyle. All other religious writings in Hinduism are derived from the Vedas. There are four Vedas namely: Rigveda, the Yajurveda, the Samaveda and the Atharvaveda. Hindus even keep the books in glass cases because they are so honored and protected. Each of the Vedas is classified into four sections. The oldest section is the Samhitas, which is the part that contains the hymns and mantras. The Brahmanas section explains the hymns and contains ritualistic teachings. The Aranyakas teaches meditation techniques and how meditation helps you forget about your problems and focus only on the universal soul. The fourth section, Upanishads, talks about our individual souls. These sections were actually rewritten into entirely new books called Upanishads. They are supposed to be end part of the Vedas or conclusions. There are more than 200 Upanishads. The Upanishads teaches people about the nature of Atman, which means their individual soul. It also teaches about the universal soul of Brahman and how the two souls connect to each other. The earliest Upanishads text references the theory of reincarnation and how the individual soul leaves the physical body after it dies and goes into a new body. This theory of reincarnation is one of the most fundamental beliefs of Hinduism that is still alive today.

The Rig-Veda in Sanskrit

Some Hindu schools teach people about other holy books that were written years after the Vedas called "Smriti" such as the Ramayana which is a holy book that emphasizes the story about Lord Rama and his wife, Sita. The demon king, Ravana, kidnapped Sita, but then was eventually rescued by her husband Rama and the monkey God named Hanuman. The story is actually a long poem (called epic poetry) and tries to give the message that goodness always triumphs over evil forces. Rama and Sita are viewed as role models as not just the perfect husband and wife, but a reflection of how true love and devotion to your spouse will always win in the end. The other Hindu epic is the Mahabharata considered as the longest epic in the world. Mahabharata can be translated as the "Great story of India". It is a story of the Kaurava and the Pandava princes over the kingdom of Hastinapura. One of the main stories of the Mahabharata is the Bhagavad Gita, a dialogue between Pandava prince Arjuna and his friend and charioteer Krishna. Krishna reveals many of the philosophies of Hinduism. These Smritis are thought to have been written by sages and do not have divine origins.

The Puranas are books that feature collections of ancient Hindu tales and praises of the various Gods and their incarnations. There are 18 main Puranas. These books help followers better understand the traditions and how Hinduism got to be where it is today. However, all the books link back to the Vedas because that was the basis for all the teachings. The only thing that separates some Hindu followers from each other is their interpretations of the text.

Chapter 18
The Mahabharata

The Mahabharata is an ancient Hindu text described as an epic written in Sanskrit. It is actually a poem, which many scholars consider to be the longest poem ever written. There are over 100,000 couplets and 200,000 verses, which is huge for just one poem. In all, there are around 1.8 million words which make it ten times longer than the Odyssey or the Iliad. Hinduism has two major Sanskrit poems; one being the Mahabharata and the other called the Ramayana. The Mahabharata is actually four times longer than the Ramayana. Scholars have often considered the Mahabharata to be just as important to the world as the Holy Bible or any of the works by Shakespeare. Unfortunately, only those within the Hindu religion are aware of its existence.

Statue of Arjuna and Krishna as his charioteer during the Kurukshetra war.

Mahabharata is basically a narrative that talks about the Kurukshetra war and the feud between two sets of paternal cousins; the Pandavas and the Kauravas. These were the five sons of King Pandu and the one hundred sons of King Dhritarashtra. King Pandu eventually dies and King Dhritarashtra became blind. These two sets of cousins became bitter rivals because they both wanted to take possession of the kingdom of Hastinapura, which ancestral significance to both sides of the family. The kingdom of Hastinapura was located on the Ganga River of northern India. After they have their battle at the field of Kurukshetra in North Delhi, the Kauravas were all killed. As for the Pandava brothers, they survived. The story involves many personal conflicts amongst the characters as well as personal agendas that each character tries to pursue. Furthermore, it consists of numerous subplots and plot twists that make it a very engaging story that is actually entertaining. But this story only makes up one fifth of the entire book. The rest of it includes myths and legends about other Hindu figures, like Bhishma, Nala and Damayanti, and the legend of Savitri.

Mahabharata is considered to be the main source of information that describes the development of Hinduism between 400 B.C. and 200 A.D. You could call it the encyclopedia of its time because it did include factual statements about the principles of the Hindu religion, moral laws and ethical science. The stories were then told through poetry to represent these principles. Together it all creates a series of Hindu fables, culture and codes of conduct that all Hindus live by. Even though the poem in the book is telling a mythological story, Hindus regard it as a book about the history of Hinduism and dharma, which is the moral law of the religion. The present day version of Mahabharata is the same one that has been used by Hindus for the past 1600 years. Although the story in the text may be considered fiction by some, it still teaches a valuable lesson to people about the evolution of Hinduism and how it relates with other types of religions.

In modern times, the Mahabharata helped influence and inspire many of India's pioneers and key figures, like Mahatma Gandhi, to push for the Indian Independence Movement. The poems have even inspired modern day poets and artists from its stories and messages. There have been theories that more than one person wrote it or that multiple people's poems were gathered together to form this collection of poetry. But it is generally thought that the Mahabharata was written by a sage called Vyasa. Since there are many sections to the book that go beyond the initial story of the cousins, this theory may have some truth to it. But to modern day Hindus, they don't care who wrote it because the important messages from the book have been passed down for thousands of years now. It is the one true Hindu bible right up there with the Vedas.

Chapter 19
Bhagavad Gita

The Bhagavad Gita often referred as simply the Gita is a 700 verse scripture. It is a major part and a principle story of the Mahabharata. It is hence an Upanishad although some say that it's a "sruti". The Gita is composed of 18 chapters in Sanskrit and each chapter is named as a "yoga" as it is supposed to spiritually train the mind and the body. The Gita is considered as one of greatest spiritual books of all times. It is in the verses of the Gita that Krishna gives out the nature of the soul and self – realization and how a person can connect with God.

Fight between Arjuna and Karna by Ramanarayanadatta Astri (Public Domain image US).

The Mahabharata as mentioned previously is a war between the Pandava and Kaurava brothers for the throne of the kingdom of Hastinapura. Yudhishtira, the eldest of the Pandavas is the rightful heir to the throne and he wants to establish himself as the king. But Duryodhana (the eldest of the Kauravas) has not only refused to give them any land but also has tried to insult the wife of the Pandavas, the beautiful Draupadi by taking her clothes off in the full durbar (or court). This has led the Pandavas to go to war with the Kauravas to revenge the humiliation of their wife but also to claim what is rightfully theirs. The battle is now between right and wrong and whole of the entire Bharat (India) is to take part in the war and hence called the Mahabaharata or Great War of India.

When the battle at the Kurukshetra is about to take place, Arjuna one of the Pandava brothers asks Krishna (his friend and charioteer) to take him to the middle of the two assembled armies so that he could see who's who. Krishna does what Arjuna has asked. This is where Arjuna has a kind of panic attack. He sees his family members and friends from on both sides, he sees his grandfather Bhisma on the Kaurava side and he refuses to fight. He questions the war and begins to lament. This is where Krishna who is the incarnation of Vishnu talks to convince Arjuna to take up arms and fight for justice, right and wrong, for dharma and to fulfill his duty as a warrior and end the injustice of Duryodhana.

Let's take a look at each of the chapters in short.

Chapter 1: The distress of Arjuna (Arjuna–Visada yoga): In this opening chapter, the two armies of Pandavas and the Kauravas are assembled at Kurukshetra. Dhritarashtra, the father of Kauravas is not sure if his sons will win so he asks his assistant Sanjaya who has a special gift to describe the scene on the battlefield. Arjuna in the meantime gets unsettled and is overcome by grief by seeing his relatives, friends and teachers in both the armies. He gives up the determination to fight.

Chapter 2: Book of doctrines (Sankhya yoga): This chapter is a like a summary of the entire Gita. Krishna reminds Arjuna of his duty to fight for right and wrong. Arjuna submits himself to Krishna as his disciple. Krishna then goes on to distinguish between the body and the soul, he explains the transmigration of the soul and how the soul can be liberated by doing deeds and attain moksha.

Chapter 3: Virtue in work (Karma yoga). Krishna explains the important of karma (doing things). One can attain moksha by doing deeds selflessly and for the pleasure of the Supreme Being. Krishna says that one should leave the results to the lord. By doing this, the doer will gain knowledge of the soul and the Supreme Being.

Chapter 4: Of the religion of knowledge (Gyaana–Karma-Sanyasa yoga): In this chapter, Krishna talks about the history of Gita and its importance. He says that he first gave the knowledge of the Gita to Vivasvan, the Sun God who then gave it to his decedents who then imparted the knowledge to the rest of humanity. He says that whenever dharma and righteousness declines, he reincarnates to impart this knowledge and preserve dharma and hence protect the good.

Chapter 5: Of religion by renouncing fruit of works (Karma–Sanyasa yoga): This chapter talks about the paths of knowledge. Arjuna is confused as to which method is better; the renunciation of work or work in devotion and Krishna advises that devotion is better. Anyone who does their work and is not attached to the worldly pleasures will find eternal happiness.

Chapter 6: Of religion of self-restraint (Dhyan yoga or Atmasanyam yoga): Anyone can control their minds and realize the Supreme Being. Other activities such as sleep, eat, work, recreation etc can be controlled and one can archive "samadhi" and realize the supreme head of God or Krishna consciousness.

Chapter 7: Of religion by discernment (Gyaana–ViGyaana yoga): Krishna is the Supreme God and ultimate truth. He describes that he is everything. Those who are advanced souls realize him and those who are not worship demigods.

Chapter 8: Of religion by devotion to the one supreme God (Aksara–Brahma yoga): Arjuna asks about Brahman and what happens at the time of death. Krishna explains that one can attain him by remembering him particularly at the time of death.

Chapter 9: Of religion by the kingly knowledge and the kingly mystery (Raja-Vidya-Raja-Guhya yoga): Krishna tells Arjuna that getting to heaven is not moksha. He explains how everything is created, maintained and preserved by him.

Chapter 10: Of religion by the heavenly perfections (Vibhuti–Vistara–yoga): Krishna says that everything is "Bhagwan" (God). All pursuits are the pursuit of Bhagwan. He says that he is the cause of all causes and specifies his manifestations. He is the object of worship for all human beings.

Chapter 11: Of the manifesting of the one and manifold (Visvarupa–Darsana yoga): In this chapter, Arjuna asks Krishna to show his real self. Krishna reveals himself as the entire universe and his infinite form. Arjuna is scared but at the same time he is in awe. He apologies and offers his salutations.

Chapter 12: Of the religion of faith (Bhakti yoga): The word "Bhakti" means devotion to Ishvara or God. Krishna talks about the devotion to God. He talks about the types of spiritual disciplines and types of devotion.

Chapter 13: Of religion by separation of matter and spirit (Ksetra–Ksetrajna Vibhaga yoga): In this chapter, Krishna talks about purusha and prakriti, the two different aspects of Brahman. Krishna talks about the differences between the physical body and the immortal soul. He also gives information about the individual souls and the ultimate supreme soul (Brahman).

Chapter 14: Of religion by separation from the qualities (Gunatraya–Vibhaga yoga): In this chapter, Krishna talks about "gunas" or quality of material nature. Krishna talks about the creation, the universe, prakriti and the gunas. He gives information about passion, goodness and lack of knowledge. He says that one should remove ignorance and live the life of goodness.

Chapter 15: Of religion by attaining the supreme (Purusottama yoga): Krishna says that God is omnipotent, omniscient and omnipresent. He says that the ultimate goal of Vedic knowledge is to free oneself from materialistic attachment and understand Lord Krishna.

Chapter 16: Of the separateness of the divine and the demonic (Daivasura–Sampad–Vibhaga yoga): Krishna talks about the two types of nature; the righteous and demonic. Those who are demonic and live without following the scriptures get lower births, while those with divine qualities acquire spirituality and perfection.

Chapter 17: Of religion by the threefold kinds of faith (Sraddhatraya-Vibhaga yoga): Krishna describes the types of faith or "shraddha" that arises from the three elements or modes of material nature. The three qualities of nature that is also present in the human mind refer to tamas, rajas, and sattva. Activities done in goodness leads to purity and devotion to Krishna while activities done in ignorance leads to materialistic pleasure which is not permanent.

Chapter 18: Of religion by deliverance and renunciation (Moksha–Sanyasa yoga): This chapter is a conclusion of the other chapters. Krishna describes the meaning of renunciation and that one can surrender everything to God. Krishna says that one can surrender to him and he will release them from karma. Basically this chapter summarizes the sense of the Vedas.

As you can see, the Bhagavad Gita is an essential part of Hindu philosophy. It details about karma, how to maintain dharma, details the nature of the soul, super soul (Supreme Being or Brahman), how to perform bhakti (devotion), about materialist attachment, and how to attain moksha by believing in Krishna. Krishna talks about how to gain liberation, get enlightenment, become free from suffering and understand the knowledge of the true self.

Chapter 20
The Ramayana

The Ramayana is one of the two major books of poetry of the Hindus. The other book is the Mahabharata, which is considered to be the longest book ever written. As for the Ramayana, it gives insight into what life was like in India during the era of 1000 B.C. The life of the characters in the story reflects the moral law of Hinduism, the dharma. The main character of the story is Rama (the seventh avatar of Lord Vishnu), an Indian prince who devoted his whole life to dharma. This is part of the reason why Indians still consider Rama to be their hero and idolize him for his ethical ideals. Rama is first described in the book as the perfect young boy and son. Then as he grew up he married his faithful and loving wife, Sita, and became the perfect husband to her. Most of all, he was a responsible ruler of the Indian city of Ayodhya and never abused his power. For the last 2000 years, Indians have been taught to act just like Rama and Sita.

The Ramayana is often played on stages in the form of dance.

The first version of Ramayana was a poem made up of 24,000 couplets, which many believe was written by the well known poet of Sanskrit known as Valmiki. In fact he was one of the first Sanskrit poets to ever exist. Legend has it that Valmiki was originally a robber who met up with a hermit one day that changed his life forever. Instead of being a cheat and a liar, this hermit turned Valmiki into an ethical and virtuous person. Then when he went to write the Ramayana, the Goddess of wisdom, Saraswati was by his side the entire time helping him visualize all of the events for the epic. This is just one more reason why the Ramayana is held in such high regards because it had a Goddess overseeing it with the author.

*Rama with wife Sita and brother Lakshmana in the forest.
Depiction by Raja Ravi Varma c.1910's.*

For centuries, the story was only told to others through word-of-mouth. Historians believe the complete version was finally written down sometime during the beginning of the Common Era, which is known to modern people as after the alleged birth of Jesus Christ. But the original written version no longer exists because it has been retold, rewritten, and retranslated countless times throughout southern Asia. People have even adapted the Ramayana into other artistic forms like puppet shows, theatrical performances, dances, movies and songs. If you ever look at the library of movies in Asia then you will find a lot of their stories referring to the Rama of the Ramayana.

The word "Ramayana" means "The march of Rama." This march it refers to is the march of someone who searches for human values. It contains a nice blend of storytelling and references to the ancient Vedic Sanskrit that Hindus take so seriously. The Hindus teach the Ramayana to their youth as sort of a way to help them become a better person and do good deeds, which is the goal of all Hindus. Since Rama was such a perfect character in every way, it is easy to make him someone to idolize. Most Indians who go to school learn about the characters and events of this story, whether they are Hindu or not. The whole Indian culture feels the stories of the Ramayana contain all the ethical ideals that one should possess in life. These teachings are also emphasized in other Indian and Southern Asian religions such as Buddhism, Sikhism and Jainism. These religions have developed their own versions of the story to better reflect their own teachings. These versions are basically rewritings of the original book which ultimately change the story of Rama. But the one thing everyone can agree on is that the story is derived from ancient Sanskrit poetry.

The story of Ramayana is of valor, ideology, devotion, loyalty, love, commitment, duty, karma and of dharma. Here's the summary of the story. Rama marries the beautiful Sita in a ceremony called Swayamvara that was organized by her father. When Rama comes of age, Kaikeyi one the wives of Dashratha (Rama's father) wants her son Bharata to become to king of Ayodhya and asks Dashratha to banish Rama for 14 years of exile in the forest. On his death bed, he obeys her command and banishes Rama. Rama being an ideal son did not refuse and decides to go. Although Rama wants go alone, his wife Sita and half-brother Lakshmana goes with him and lives in the forest. In the meantime, Bharata although heartbroken by his mother's misdeeds he becomes king of Ayodhya. Bharata goes to the forest and pleads with Rama to come back. Rama declines and says he cannot break his vow. Bharata goes back but takes Rama's sandals and places it on the throne as a symbol of Rama's authority over the kingdom. While Rama, Sita and Lakshmana are spending their time in the forest, Ravana the king of Lanka (current day Sri Lanka) abducts Sita and takes her to Lanka and tries to marry her. When Rama finds out he decides to go to Lanka and free his wife. Lord Hanuman who in fact is incarnation of Lord Shiva helps Rama. The army of Rama now proceeds to Lanka. While in Lanka, Hanuman pleads with Ravana to free Sita and when he refuses, he burns the entire Lanka with his tail. A battle takes place and Ravana is killed. Sita is reunited with Rama. After 14 years of exile, they go back to Ayodhya. Rama establishes a kingdom where all his subjects live in happiness.

Ram (middle), Sita and brother Lakshman

The epic is divided into 7 books called "kandas" that describe the life of Rama in detail. They are:

Book on the childhood of Rama- Bala Kanda
Book of Ayodhya - Ayodhya Kanda
Book of the forest - Araṇya Kanda
Book of the monkey heroes - Kishkindha Kanda
Book of beauty - Sundara Kanda
Book of war - Lanka Kanda or Yuddha Kanda
Last book of Ramayana - Uttara Kanda

Chapter 21
River Ganges in the Hindu religion

The River Ganges is considered to be one of the holiest rivers in the world because it holds significance with many religions of the eastern world. To Hindus, it holds the most significance. The River Ganges is often referred to as Ganga which actually means that it emanates from the lotus feet of the lord. The main source of the river is a glacier called "Gangotri," which is in the Indian Himalayas and is around 4,000 meters above sea level. This river alone provides 25% of India's total water supply to its citizens. But this is not why it is worshipped as a sacred river. In Hinduism, Ganga is thought of as a deity. Hindus even give it the godly name "Ganga Maiya," which means Mother Ganga. The Ganga name only appears twice in the ancient Vedic texts. Ganga wasn't even referred to as a Goddess until many years after the Vedic was written.

Hindus taking a dip in the holy Ganges: They believe that their sins will be washed away in the river and attain moksha.

Legend has it that Ganga was in love with Lord Krishna while in heaven. Lord Krishna was already devoted to another lover named Radha, so he could not return the same feelings for Ganga. However, Ganga's devotion to Lord Krishna made Radha jealous, so she plotted against Ganga by putting a curse on her that she would fall on earth as a river. Krishna made her realize that Ganga is just an extension of herself in the form of liquid. Once she realized this, she made Ganga sit near Lord Krishna and blessed her that Ganga would flow on earth as a river of water for all eternity. This is why the river is so sacred because it possesses the spirit of Ganga. Most of the spiritual beliefs surrounding the River Ganga come from myths associated with the Goddess. Hindus think of Mother

Ganga as a beautiful woman who holds a water lily and water pot in her hands, a white crown on her head and rides a crocodile. Any rituals held near the Ganga River are said to be more sacred and blessed. Also, holding water from the river in your hands is sacred as well. Hindus are not supposed to lie or cheat when they have water from the sacred river in their hands. Hindus also sprinkle this water in their homes and on auspicious occasions for purification purposes. In the ancient Hindu texts the "Puranas," the scriptures indicate that the name, sight and touch of anything Ganga will cleanse your sins away. If you were to go for a swim in the river then you would be given heavenly blessings by the Gods above, especially by Mother Ganga.

There is another legend on the descent of Ganga from the heavens to earth. There was a king called Sagar and he wanted to be the emperor of the whole of India so he performed Ashwamedha Yagna a horse ritual to prove his supremacy. Indra, God of rain stole the horse and tied it in the ashram of a sage called Kapila who was in deep meditation. When the army of Sagar got to the ashram, Kapila woke up from his mediation and angrily started killing the sons of Sagar. The only way to save them was by bringing Ganga from the heavens to purify Kapila. Ganga was eventually persuaded by Lord Brahma to flow down to earth but she was not happy so started flowing rapidly on earth destructively. Lord Shiva said that earth will not be able to sustain the descent of Ganga like this so he tied Ganga to his hair so that she could go down gently. Hence the Ganga is considered as an attribute of Lord Shiva. That is why you will see Ganga flowing from the matted hair of Lord Shiva.

The land located next to the River Ganga is considered to be hallowed ground. Hindus believe if you die on this land next to the river then you will reach a heavenly place and all of your sins will disappear. If a deceased person were to be cremated and have their ashes scattered in this river then their soul would be salvaged. Hindu families in India often use the Ganga Ghats of holy city of Varanasi to perform the cremations and funerals of their departed loved ones. Besides it being a place for deceased people, it is truly a place for living people as well. In fact the Ganga Dashami festival takes place every summer. This is where Hindus take a dip in the river allowing the Goddess to wipe away their sins. It is kind of like a yearly cleansing ritual that Hindus like to go through in order to stay pure. Hindus during this festival will also light lamps and incense as a way to worship and please the Goddess. They also make an offering of flowers, sandalwood or milk to Ganga in exchange for blessedness.

The Hindu teachings of the River Ganges have varied meanings because of the different myths and legends that have been taught over the years. Many of these teachings were only done orally, so for centuries there were no scriptures or texts that people could study or read from. So no one really knows which parts of the tale are true and which ones are not true. Either way, the river is still a special place for all Hindus and they each get something special from being there. Many of pilgrimage sites of the Hindus lie on the holy banks of the Ganges some of which include Varanasi, Haridwar, Gangotri, Haridwar and Allahabad.

Chapter 22
The cow in Hindu religion

The cow is a respected animal in Hinduism. They are not supposed to be mistreated or killed, unless it is performed in a ritual sacrifice. In India, cows are often allowed to roam free on the streets and in towns. They have been known to hold up traffic simply because wild cows wander into the roads. This freedom that cows have in India goes back to the Hindu religion where they are valued. People in the western part of the world don't understand this because to them cows are nothing more than a supply of hamburger meat. They also think Hindus worship their cows and think of them as Gods, which is not true. Cows are not thought of as Gods nor are they worshiped. They are just respected and allowed to have their freedom. Some might say this is a worse life because the cows are homeless and have no one to supply them with food. Sometimes Hindus from nearby temples will care for the cows out of courtesy for their well being. But, they won't eat them or raise them as livestock. Many of these temples are bull temples where they respect all male cattle, particularly the Nandi Bull. The two most notable temples for this bull are at the Shiva temple in Mahabalipuram and the "Dodda Basavana Gudi" (or just the Nandhi Temple) in Bangalore.

The ancient Indian scriptures of Hinduism show that cows were revered even thousands of years ago. Bulls and oxen were occasionally slaughtered in a sacrifice to the Gods, and then their meat was eaten. However, cows that produced milk were not allowed to be sacrificed. Some verses from the Vedic Sanskrit refer to the cow as the Goddess Devi. Eventually, eating cow meat was permitted but the Vedic scriptures did not recommend it. Instead they recommended that people practice vegetarianism because abstaining from eating meat brings great rewards from the gods. But by the time Buddhism and Jainism came around, the Hindus opinions on eating meat changed and so they stopped once again. Some historians suggest there were practical reasons in addition to spiritual reasons for them refraining from eating meat. For one thing, slaughtering cows at a religious sacrifice or ritual was very expensive. Cows produced many more products besides meat, such as browned butter (ghee), curd, milk and dried dung for cooking. Many believe Jainism influenced Hinduism on strict vegetarian lifestyles.

Cows are considered as sacred animals. Hindus do not eat their meat.

In modern times, most Hindus still do not eat beef from a cow. This is generally due to both religious and economic reasons. Even the notable Indian, Mahatma Gandhi, could not stand the way cows were being treated. This is out of respect to the animal more than anything. As for regular Hindu families, they typically have one dairy cow in their possession. They love the cow the same way that Americans love their dogs or cats. Indians even treat cows as members of their family. Furthermore, the products cows produce are also held sacred. Milk helps children grow big and strong, and cow dung has become a major energy source for many Indian families. They see these products as a gift from the cow to mankind. And once a year, there is a special cow festival called Gopastami. This is a day when stray cows on the streets are washed up and then brought to temples where they are decorated. Then they are given special offerings in exchange for the gift of life that they give to people with the products they produce. Cows themselves may also be offered as gifts between Hindu families, especially poor families that have nothing else to part with. You could say that cows are adored and loved by Hindus.

Chapter 23
Major Hindu Festivals

India is known as the land of festivals. Let's take a look at some of the popular Hindu festivals.

Durga Puja celebration, the annual worship of Goddess Durga. A temporary stage called a pandal is erected and devotees pray in front of the idol of Durga.

Diwali is one of the biggest Hindu festivals. It is known as the festival of lights, which visually makes it the brightest and biggest festival out of all the other Hindu festivals. The lights are supposed to give respect to the heavens above and all the joy and prosperity they bring to life on earth. This celebration lasts approximately four days, so if you come to India during these four days then you will see lots of bright lights all around the country. Throughout these four days of celebration, there are different traditions that are celebrated. But, what is celebrated the most is life in general and the joy of being alive. The historical background of Diwali goes all the way back to ancient India when it was a harvest festival. Some Hindu legends even state that Diwali was really the celebration of Lord Vishnu and Lakshmi getting married. Others believe it is a day dedicated to worshipping the dark Goddess of strength, Mother Kali. Many worship Lakshmi, the Goddess of wealth. It is also thought that Lord Ram came back to this kingdom of Ayodhya after spending 14 years of banishment. To Hindus, it really depends which story of Diwali they wish to believe in. But no matter what, they all celebrate it on the same four days of the year which typically occur between October 16th and November 15th. Diwali is also considered to be the Hindu New Year as well.

Holi is known as the festival of colors and love, which is an extremely fun event that is lively and entertaining. This Hindu festival treats people with music, dance, games and other fun activities. But the best attraction to see is all the bright colors of the festival. Holi occurs right at the beginning of spring. It is a way for people to say goodbye to the harshness of the winter season and enjoy a new season of warmth and beauty. More importantly, this is when people harvest crops and fills their households with food for the season. Holi is an ancient Hindu festival that has become popular with many people across South Asia, even non-Hindus. Holi references a symbolic legend that signifies the use of color at the festival. The word Holi comes from the word Holika, who was actually the evil sister of the demon king named Hiranyakashipu. The demon king was eventually killed by fire, which also burnt Holika. A bonfire is used to represent the death of the demon king and a victory for the good spirits that killed her. So by celebrating the defeat of evil, it becomes a celebration of love instead. Then over the years, colors were used to further signify the defeat of these evil forces.

Durga Puja is a festival celebrated in autumn for 10 days and 9 nights. During these 10 days, Hindus gather together for rituals, feasts, fasts, dancing and singing. All of this is to honor Goddess Durga, who is known in Hinduism as the Supreme Mother Goddess. The 9 nights of the festival are known as Navaratri, which represents a celebration of good over evil. This refers to the Goddess Durga ridding the world of Mahishasura, who was an evil buffalo demon. His mother was a she buffalo named Mahishi and his father was Rambha. The nine days of Navaratri are divided into three sets of three day festivities in honor of Durga. During the first three days, Durga is called upon as a powerful force to destroy all defects and impurities in the world. The next three days consist of honoring the Goddess for giving spiritual wealth to all her followers and devotees. The last three days is when people worship Durga as the Goddess of wisdom, Saraswati. Hindus believe that all three aspects of Durga need to be celebrated in order to have a successful and happy life. After nine days of celebrating, they will have achieved this goal. The celebrations end with Dusshera and Vijayadashami.

A Harry Potter rakhi: Sisters would tie one of these rakhis on their brother's hand and brothers would vow to protect them.

Makar Sankranti (or Pongal in South India) is a popular harvest festival celebrated all over India. It is supposed to mark the movement of the sun into the zodiac sign of Makar rashi (or Capricorn).

Saraswati puja is another festival where Saraswati, the Goddess of wisdom, art and education is worshipped. She is also worshiped on Vasant Panchmi or the fifth day of spring.

Maha Shivaratri is the day when Lord Shiva got married to Parvati. For the Hindus Maha Shivaratri is an important festival of Lord Shiva. Hindus sing praise and chant mantras in his honor.

Janmashtami is the day of the birth of Krishna, the avatar of Vishnu. Many Hindus fast on fruits and refrain from eating grains. Krishna was born in Mathura town in Western Uttar Pradesh. Hindus stay up all night and sing bhajans in praise of Krishna.

Rama Navami is a very popular festival in India. It is supposed to be the birth of Lord Rama, the seventh avatar of Vishnu. Devotees read the epic Ramayana and sing bhajans in praise of Rama.

Hanuman Jayanti is the day of the birth of Lord Hanuman.

Raksha Bandhan is a festival to denote the love between sisters and brothers. The sister would tie a rakhi on the hand of their brother and the brother would vow to protect her. It's quite a joyous occasion and people from all faiths celebrate this festival particularly in the northern parts of India.

Some children celebrate the birth of Krishna by getting him a cake.

Ganesh Chaturthi is celebrated to honor Lord Ganesha. It is a very popular in the state of Maharashtra. Devotees would sing bhajans in honor of Ganesha.

Chapter 24
Important Hindu Holy places to visit in India

India still attracts tourists who are interested in historical Indian culture, particularly culture related to Hinduism. The holy places of Hinduism are of particular interest to people. The most famous holy place of Hinduism is Varanasi (Banaras). It is located on the banks of the Ganga, which is the famous Ganges River of India. It is about 450 miles south from the city of Delhi. Varanasi is an ancient city that is said to be one of the oldest cities in the entire world. All of the ancient Indian Sanskrit and texts refer to Varanasi as the "foremost city of Shiva." One of the most popular temples of Varanasi is the "Kashi Vishwanath Mandir" one of the holiest of the Shiva temples. The original temple was destroyed when India was ruled by the Mughals but later rebuilt. Modern day Hindus typically retire in Varanasi when they get older because they want to seek liberation before they die. That is why the city has plenty of cremation ghats. This is where dead bodies are cremated. Families often take the ashes of their loved ones and scatter them into the Ganga River because they feel it will bring salvations to the departed soul.

Another ancient Indian city is Mathura, which is only 95 miles away from Delhi. Hindus recognize this city as the birth place of the Lord Krishna. The Kesava Deo Temple is the main temple, which is a place devoted to worshipping Krishna and Radha. The rest of the city contains many holy sites and sacred forests, which are called Vraj. It is thought that Krishna spent his childhood here. When Hindus visit this city they often want to go to the village of Vrindavan, which is where

Krishna lived. Now the village is a town with over five thousand temples, all devoted to Krishna. This city is also a popular retirement city for elderly Hindus because they hope they will return from death to spend eternity with the lord.

For those interested in Shakta holy sites, Kanyakumari is a town in southern India that you will want to check out. The main attraction there is the temple devoted to Parvati, the wife of Shiva. What is particularly interested about Kanyakumari is that it contains the Bay of Bengal, which is located between the Indian and Arabian oceans. Many pilgrims and Hindus come to the Bay of Bengal to bathe. The sand on the beaches has seven different colors. Legend says that the sand changed colors because of the seven colors of rice that was thrown at this spot during the celebration of Shiva marrying Parvati.

An ancient Hindu tradition known as Smartas (those who are experts in Smirtis) reside in the city of Puri. The people who live in this community follow Shankaracharya, who created four seats in the four holiest places in India. Shankaracharya is the head of the monastery, which still exists today. The current one resides in Puri, which is a city located in the Indian state of Odisha located towards the east coast. The city contains a 900 year old Vishnu temple called Jagannath Mandir, who is considered to be the lord of the universe. It contains 6000 priests and holds chariot festival every year. It is truly quite a site to see.

Gaya in Bihar state is another holy site in India of mythological significance. It has a Vishnupad temple frequented by the people of state and India. It is also a site where Hindus pray for their ancestors on the banks of the Phalgu River. Just a few kilometers away is the town of Bodh Gaya where Buddha got his enlightenment.

The Vishnupad Temple in the town of Gaya, Bihar.

The Himalayan "char dham" namely Badrinath, Kedarnath, Gangotri, and Yamunotri are very much revered by the Hindus. Millions of Hindus make their pilgrimages to these four sites every year. It is said that those who visit these places have their sins washed away and free them from the recycle of birth. You can find out more information on the char dhams here http://www.shalusharma.com/char-dham-yatra. Ancient city of Haridwar situated in the state of Uttarakhand is another holy pilgrimage site of the Hindus of historical and mythological significance. It is here where the River Ganges enters the Indo-Gangetic planes of North India.

Badrinath Temple Entrance

There are many holy places in the eyes of Hindus. A holy place is basically somewhere that has a historical significance with a God or Goddess in Hinduism. Either that or it is a place where religious leaders come together to share sacred stories and practice Hindu traditions with other people. If you are a tourist then you will definitely want to visit the temples of these ancient Indian cities. Some of these temples are older than any building or structure in the developed world where you come from. Perhaps going to these places will give you a sense of the divine energy that inhibits them.

For more travel information and places to visit in India: http://www.shalusharma.com

Chapter 25
Tips for visiting a Hindu temple

If you are considering visiting a Hindu temple then here are some tips.

Wear modest clothing

It is highly recommended that you wear modest clothing. If you are wearing jeans and tops, it is absolutely fine, you will not be prevented from entering temples but most Hindu women prefer to wear sarees and salwar kameez when visiting temples. Men usually wear kurta pajamas but again jeans and shirts or t-shirts are absolutely fine.

Cover your head

Although this is not really necessary in most temples in India but some women prefer to cover their head with their "dupatta". If you aren't wearing the traditional Indian salwaar kameej then there is no need to cover your head.

Don't eat meat a few days before your visit

Many Hindus prefer not to eat meat if they happen to be visiting an important temple particularly if they are going on a pilgrimage to places such as Varanasi or Kumbh Mela. You might consider refraining from eating meat a day or two before going to the temple.

Balaji Temple in Birmingham, Great Britain

Take a shower before you come

Most Indians usually take a shower before they visit temples. Hindus adore their Gods and Goddess with loving sincerity and therefore prefer to cleanse their bodies before entering the holy sanctuary.

Remove your footwear

If one thing is frowned upon - it is wearing of shoes in temples. Shoes are considered unclean so you will have to take them off. Most temples have free shoe-stalls where you hand over your shoes or sandals which can be collected when you return. It may not be necessary to remove your socks.

Prostate to the deity

When you enter the temple, you fold your hands, prostate and offer your salutations or "pranaam" to the Gods and Goddesses. Some people touch the ground and then the forehead. It is like offering yourself to God. Always prostate to the Lord Ganesha the Elephant God first as he is the remover of all obstacles and he is always prayed to first. All prayers in a Hindu temple start by offering him a prayer at the start.

Sit down with legs folded

In most temples, devotees are expected to sit with their legs folded. Do not sit down with legs pointing to the deities. You can fold your hands and close your eyes. This is the time when you can prey, ask forgiveness or express your desires and wishes to God.

Don't talk during the puja

Ideally, you are not supposed to be talking when the mantras, bhajans or devotional songs are being sung. In fact, you are supposed to take part in it. If you don't know the best option is to listen and meditate.

Take the aarti

When a plate of aarti or the "sacramental lamp" is offered to you, you place both hands over it (far enough not to get burnt) and then place it on your head (symbol of purification). The Gods and Goddesses then bless you through the flame. The light from the lamp is supposed to remove darkness. Put some money in the aarti plate (only if others are doing the same thing). The money will either be taken by the priest of used for temple maintenances whatever the policy maybe of the temple you are visiting.

Take the "Prasad"

If you are offered any offerings (called the prasad) take them with your right hand while placing your left hand beneath it like a cup. The left is considered unclean as it is used mainly for washing the backside.

Take the aarti when offered. Some put money which goes to either the priest or towards the maintenance of the temple.

Remember rituals will differ from one temple to another but these are the basics. Not all Hindus even follow these rules. For instance, I know of Hindus who eat meat and visit the temple the same day. That's the great thing about Hinduism; it gives the devotee the freedom to think and practice the religion in the manner they choose fit.

Chapter 26
Conclusion

By now, you must have a pretty good understanding of Hinduism and all the history and traditions that are a part of it. It is a religion that is thousands of years old and one of the oldest religions in existence. To this day it has over 750 million followers with most of them residing in India. The reason why so many followers still exist is because of what Hinduism really stands for. It isn't just about worshipping gods or meditating for hours every day. Hinduism ultimately teaches people how to be decent human beings. It encourages people to do good deeds and not commit evil acts. Of course the reasons they teach people for being this way has to do with Samsara, which is the cycle of life and death. Hindus want to build up good karma so they can take it with them to each new life they live. Then eventually, this karma will allow them to reach the path of moksha (liberation from the recycle of birth) where they will get to spend the rest of eternity in the Kingdom of God. This is a sanctuary away from the physical world where there is no pain or sadness. There is only the realization of the one true god, Brahman. He is the universal God that is a part of all life on earth and is the reason for the existence of the universe to begin with. Hindus see Brahman and everything, which makes them understand that superficial beliefs and values mean very little. Once they realize this, they can become happier people and ultimately try to spread that happiness towards other people.

Hinduism is a unique religion because it doesn't teach its followers to worship one God or prophet. Even though Brahman is often referred to as the one true

God or Supreme Being, Hindus don't actually think of him the same way other religions think of god. Brahman is not an "old man in the sky" who listens to people's prayers and answers them. Hinduism teaches that people are responsible for their own actions, and particularly their own karma. Brahman is responsible for creating the karma that people receive from their actions. It is a cause and effect type of situation where good actions will grant good karma and bad actions will grant bad karma. Hindus have the best shot at receiving good karma because they inherit the knowledge about Brahman's existence and accept the power it gives to their soul through karma. So Hindus continuously try to achieve good karma in order to get closer to Brahman in the afterlife.

Overall, Hinduism has influenced a lot of culture around the world. Even regions of the world that don't follow Hinduism, like in the western regions, still use some of the practices derived from the Hindu religion. Yoga is a perfect example of this. People practice yoga to allow their mind, body and soul to all merge into one ultimate spiritual being. This allows them to let go of their stresses and frustrations through various types of yoga practices. Some of these practices involve physical posture movements while others involve mediation techniques. While non-Hindus use these techniques as a mere stress reliever, true Hindus use it to create good karma and to eventually reach moksha. They also use it to communicate with one of the many personal Gods. But regardless of which God they communicate with, all of the Gods have Brahman inside of them. So there is no right or wrong god to connect with through prayer. In the end, it is all about spirituality and trying to be a better person. Hopefully this book has helped you understand these primary principles of Hinduism and encouraged you to perform good deeds in your life.

You might wish to take a look at some other books.

Hinduism For Kids: Beliefs And Practices
Buddhism Made Easy: Buddhism for Beginners and Busy People
Religions of the World for Kids
Mother Teresa of Calcutta: Finding God Helping Others: Life of Mother Teresa

###

Hare Krishna, Hare Krishna, Krishna Krishna, Hare Hare
Hare Rama, Hare Rama, Rama Rama, Hare Hare